SUMMER OLYMPICS

ALL-TIME GREATS

BY ANTHONY STREETER

Book design by Jake Slavik
Cover design by Jake Slavik

Photographs ©: Rebecca Blackwell/AP Images, cover (top), 1 (top); Kyodo/AP Images, cover (bottom), 1 (bottom); Bettmann/Getty Images, 4, 9, 10; The Print Collector/Hulton Archive/Getty Images, 7; Tony Duffy/Getty Images Sport/Getty Images, 13; Clive Brunskill/Getty Images Sport/Getty Images, 15; Buda Mendes/Getty Images Sport/Getty Images, 16; Jed Jacobsohn/Getty Images Sport/Getty Images, 19; Marcel ter Bals/BSR Agency/Getty Images Sport/Getty Images, 21

Press Box Books, an imprint of Press Room Editions.

ISBN
978-1-63494-864-7 (library bound)
978-1-63494-882-1 (paperback)
978-1-63494-917-0 (epub)
978-1-63494-900-2 (hosted ebook)

Library of Congress Control Number: 2023923233

Distributed by North Star Editions, Inc.
2297 Waters Drive
Mendota Heights, MN 55120
www.northstareditions.com

Printed in the United States of America
082024

ABOUT THE AUTHOR

Anthony Streeter is a former sportswriter who has written for various newspapers. He lives in Columbia, Missouri, with his wife and three kids.

TABLE OF CONTENTS

GEREVICH

CHAPTER 1
EARLY OLYMPIC STARS

The first modern Olympics took place in 1896 in Athens, Greece. **James Connolly** left Harvard College to compete there. In his first event, he won gold in the triple jump. The Boston native went on to win two more medals in Athens. Four years later, he added another medal in Paris, France.

Hungarian fencer **Aladár Gerevich** won gold in the team sabre event in 1932. In 1960, he won that event for the sixth time in a row. No athlete in any sport has matched that feat.

Gerevich also won three individual medals. He might have won even more. However, the 1940 and 1944 Olympics were canceled due to World War II (1939–45).

FEMALE FIRSTS

Early on, women had few opportunities in the Olympics. The 1900 Games were the first to include women. Only 22 women took part. Swiss sailor Helene de Pourtales was one of them. She won a gold and a silver medal. That made her the first woman to win an Olympic gold medal.

Politics and racism overshadowed the 1936 Olympics in Berlin, Germany. But **Jesse Owens** rose above it. The Black American track star competed in four events. He won gold medals in all four. Owens set an Olympic record in the long jump. And he broke the 200-meter world record. His 4x100-meter team also set a world record. It was one of the greatest track-and-field performances ever.

American diver **Pat McCormick** failed to qualify for the 1948 Olympics. Four years later, she more than made up for it. McCormick won the women's 3-meter and 10-meter events. Then she did it again in 1956. No diver had ever done the "double-double" before.

The Soviet Union dominated women's gymnastics during this era. Soviet star **Larisa Latynina** performed her routines with grace. And she rarely made mistakes. From 1956 to

1964, she won 18 medals. No one matched Latynina's record for nearly 50 years.

Volleyball became an Olympic sport in 1964. **Masae Kasai** served as Japan's team captain that year. She and her teammates worked regular jobs all day. Then they practiced all night. They became tough and strong. Their play helped change stereotypes about Asian women. Playing on home soil in Tokyo, Kasai led Japan to the gold medal.

American swimmer **Mark Spitz** predicted he could win six gold medals in 1968. Instead, he won four medals. Two were gold, one

STAT SPOTLIGHT

OLYMPIC RECORD

MOST GOLD MEDALS BY A FEMALE ATHLETE

Larisa Latynina: 9

was silver, and one was bronze. It was a disappointing performance for Spitz. But he made up for it in 1972. This time he didn't make any predictions. He just went out and won gold in all seven of his races. Nobody had won that many gold medals in a single Olympics.

COMANECI

CHAPTER 2

ICONIC PERFORMERS

Olympic gymnastics had never seen anything like Romania's **Nadia Comaneci**. She flowed through her routine on the uneven bars. Her performance was flawless. The judges awarded her a score of 10. No gymnast had ever earned a perfect score in the Olympics. Comaneci went on to earn six more perfect 10s in the 1976 Games. In Comaneci's two Olympic appearances, she won nine medals. Five of them were gold.

The heptathlon tests track-and-field athletes across seven events. To win, athletes need to be fast and strong. They need excellent endurance. Mental toughness is important, too. **Jackie Joyner-Kersee** had it all. In 1984, the US star won a silver medal while injured. Then she claimed the next two heptathlon golds. Joyner-Kersee also earned a gold and two bronzes in the long jump.

Steve Redgrave won his first gold medal in 1984. The British rower won gold again in each of his next four Olympics. No rower had ever done that before.

STAT SPOTLIGHT

OLYMPIC AND WORLD RECORD

MOST POINTS IN A WOMEN'S HEPTATHLON

Jackie Joyner-Kersee: 7,291 (1988)

Men's basketball became an Olympic sport in 1936. A new era began in 1992. Finally, the top professional players were allowed to play for Team USA. The "Dream Team" featured a ton of stars. Fans followed their every move. No opponent came within 30 points of beating them. Of all the stars on the team, none of them played as well as **Charles Barkley**. The forward led the Dream Team in scoring. Then his play sparked another gold-medal run for Team USA in 1996.

JOYNER-KERSEE

The greatest basketball dynasty came from the US women. They won a record seventh straight gold medal in 2021. It was the fifth gold for guards **Sue Bird** and **Diana Taurasi**. They became the first basketball players to ever win five gold medals. Bird was an excellent passer and playmaker. Meanwhile, Taurasi could score from almost anywhere on the court. The United States had a perfect 38–0 Olympic record in games in which Bird and Taurasi played.

KARCH KIRALY

Karch Kiraly did just about everything in volleyball. He won a pair of Olympic gold medals with the US men's indoor team in 1984 and 1988. In 1996, he came back for the Olympic debut of beach volleyball. He won gold again. Later, Kiraly coached the US women to Olympic bronze in 2016. And in 2021, he led the US women to their first gold.

Sisters **Venus Williams** and **Serena Williams** both won Olympic gold medals in singles tennis. But the Americans were at their best when playing together. They won gold in women's doubles in 2000, 2008, and 2012. It wasn't until 2016 that they lost an Olympic doubles match. Still, Venus won silver in mixed doubles that year. That medal made her the sport's most decorated Olympian.

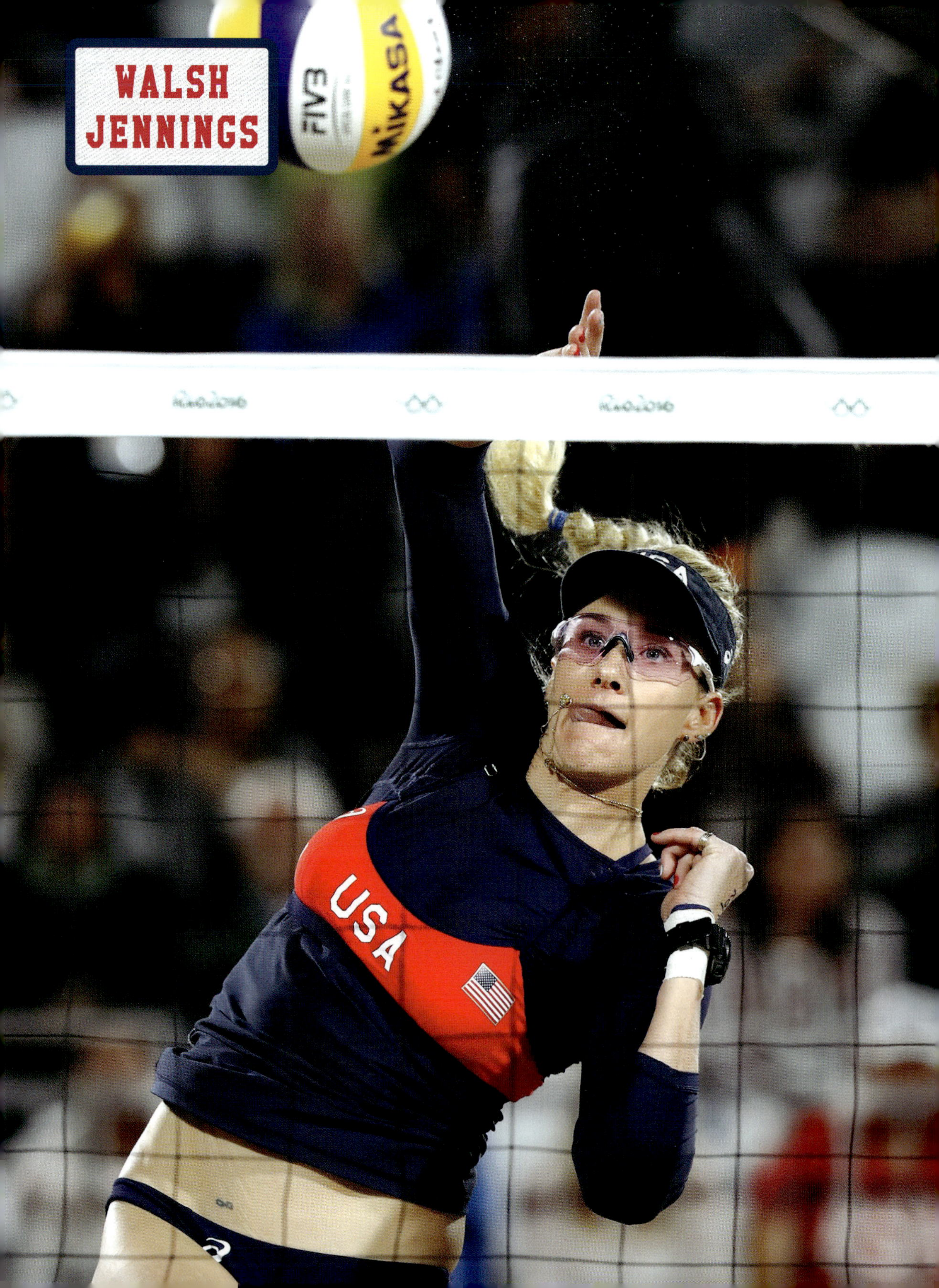
WALSH
JENNINGS
FIVB
MIKASA
Rio2016
Rio2016
USA

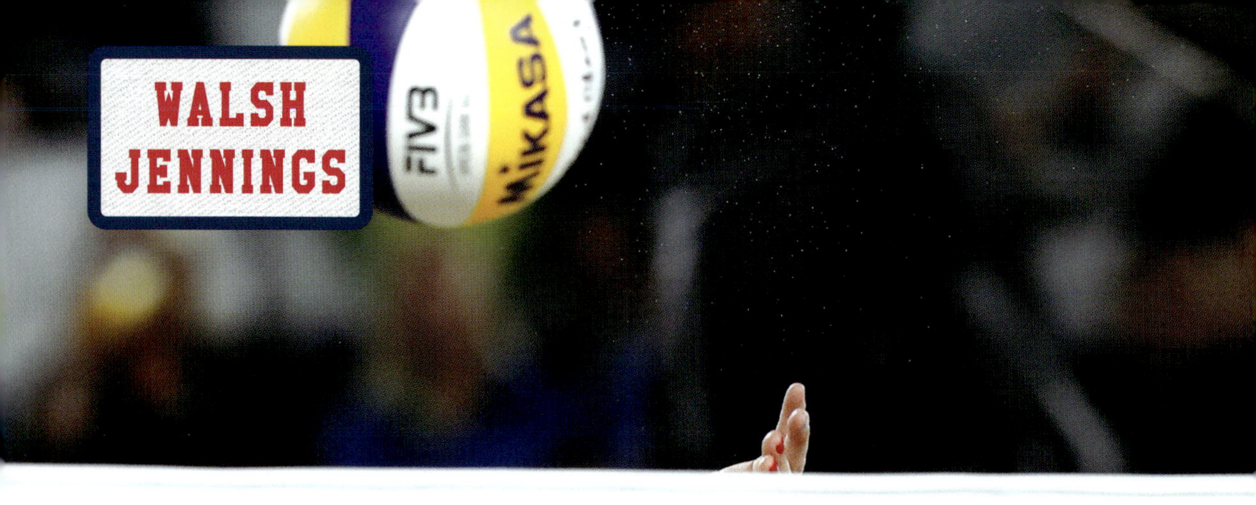

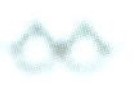

CHAPTER 3

KEEPING THE FLAME ALIVE

Kerri Walsh Jennings played with the US indoor volleyball team at the 2000 Olympics. Soon after, she partnered with **Misty May-Treanor**. No beach volleyball duo had ever been more successful. The taller Walsh Jennings dominated at the net.

STAT SPOTLIGHT

OLYMPIC RECORD

CONSECUTIVE BEACH VOLLEYBALL WINS

Misty May-Treanor and Kerri Walsh Jennings: 21

May-Treanor thrived with her versatility. In three Olympics, the duo won three gold medals. During that time, they lost just one set. Walsh Jennings added a bronze medal in 2016 with a new partner.

US swimmer **Michael Phelps** won 28 Olympic medals, and 23 of them were gold. Both are all-time records. His most memorable performance came in 2008. That year, Phelps became the first athlete in any sport to win eight gold medals at one Olympics. Seven of those performances were world records.

Usain Bolt also broke out at the 2008 Olympics. The Jamaican sprinter won the 100-meter and 200-meter races. He set world records in both. Then he won both events in 2012 and 2016. His 4x100-meter teams also won those years. Bolt was more than just fast,

though. Fans were also amused by his funny personality before and after races.

Women's wrestling became an Olympic sport in 2004. That was perfect timing for **Kaori Icho**. The Japanese star won four straight gold medals. Men first wrestled in the Olympics in 1896. Yet before Icho, no wrestler had won four golds.

Few knew of **Katie Ledecky** before the 2012 Olympics. After all, the US swimmer was only 15 years old. Winning the women's 800-meter freestyle made her a star. Longer freestyle events were her specialty. Other swimmers rarely got close to beating her. In 2021, Ledecky won her 10th medal. Only four swimmers had more.

US gymnast **Simone Biles** performed routines packed with difficulty. And few could match her technique. That combination helped

STAYING AROUND

US shooter Kim Rhode competed in her sixth Olympics in 2016. She won a medal in all six. Only a few athletes have competed in more Olympics. Canadian equestrian rider Ian Millar appeared in a record 10. Canoeist Josefa Idem-Guerrini of West Germany and Italy went to eight Games. That's the women's record. Both qualified for the last time in 2012.

her dominate the sport. At the 2016 Olympics, she won four gold medals and one bronze. Her five medals matched an American record for the sport. In 2021, she added two more medals.

No team dominated in the 2010s like the US women's water polo squad. Among its wins were Olympic gold medals in 2012, 2016, and 2021. **Maggie Steffens** led the way. She's the sport's leading scorer at the Olympics. Steffens was named Olympic Most Valuable Player two times.

TIMELINE

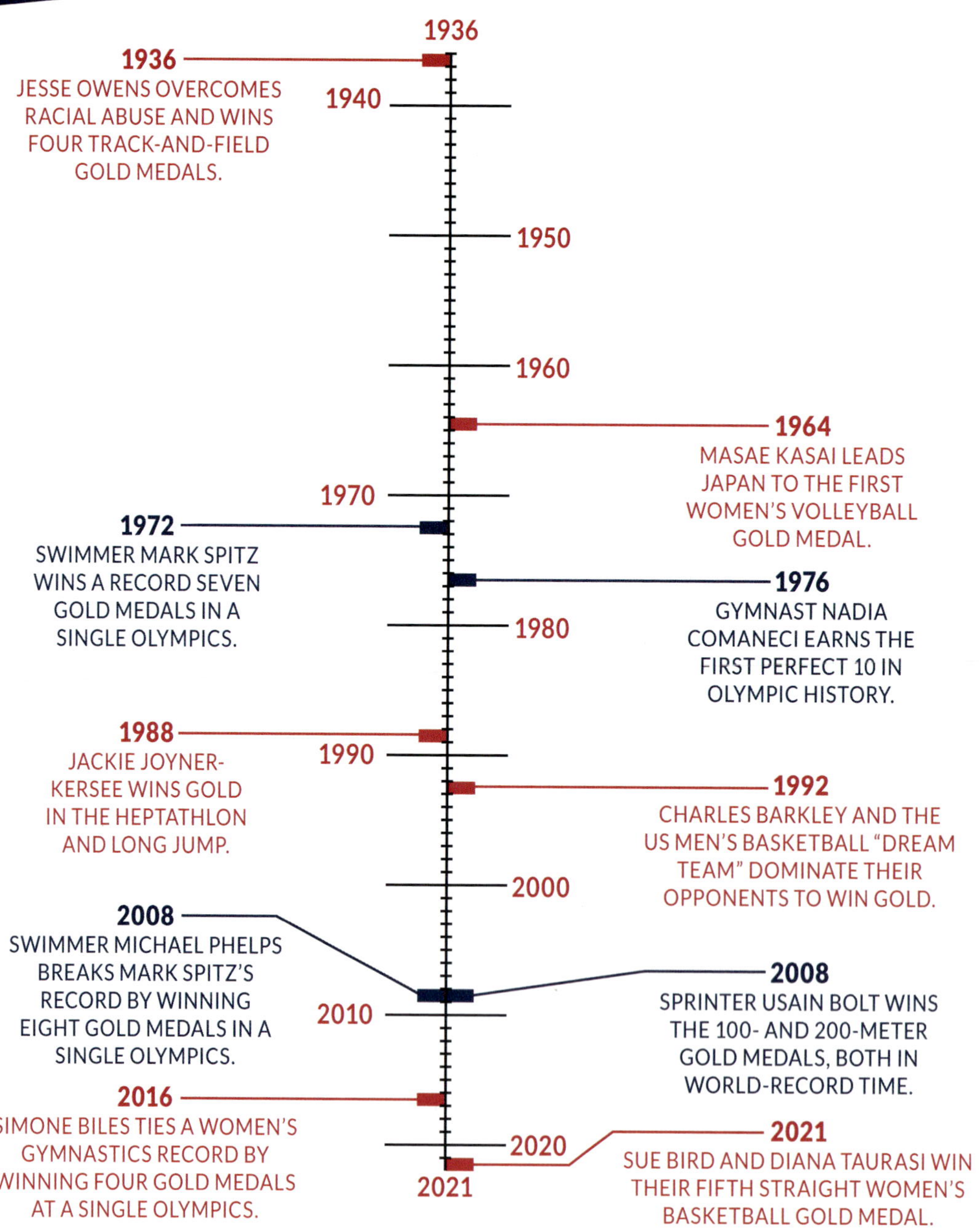

1936
JESSE OWENS OVERCOMES RACIAL ABUSE AND WINS FOUR TRACK-AND-FIELD GOLD MEDALS.

1964
MASAE KASAI LEADS JAPAN TO THE FIRST WOMEN'S VOLLEYBALL GOLD MEDAL.

1972
SWIMMER MARK SPITZ WINS A RECORD SEVEN GOLD MEDALS IN A SINGLE OLYMPICS.

1976
GYMNAST NADIA COMANECI EARNS THE FIRST PERFECT 10 IN OLYMPIC HISTORY.

1988
JACKIE JOYNER-KERSEE WINS GOLD IN THE HEPTATHLON AND LONG JUMP.

1992
CHARLES BARKLEY AND THE US MEN'S BASKETBALL "DREAM TEAM" DOMINATE THEIR OPPONENTS TO WIN GOLD.

2008
SWIMMER MICHAEL PHELPS BREAKS MARK SPITZ'S RECORD BY WINNING EIGHT GOLD MEDALS IN A SINGLE OLYMPICS.

2008
SPRINTER USAIN BOLT WINS THE 100- AND 200-METER GOLD MEDALS, BOTH IN WORLD-RECORD TIME.

2016
SIMONE BILES TIES A WOMEN'S GYMNASTICS RECORD BY WINNING FOUR GOLD MEDALS AT A SINGLE OLYMPICS.

2021
SUE BIRD AND DIANA TAURASI WIN THEIR FIFTH STRAIGHT WOMEN'S BASKETBALL GOLD MEDAL.

CHAMPIONSHIP FACTS

SUMMER OLYMPICS

First held: 1896

Most Summer Olympic medals: Michael Phelps, 28

Most Summer Olympic gold medals: Michael Phelps, 23

Most Summer Olympic medals by country: United States, 3,105

Stats are accurate through 2023.

MORE INFORMATION

To learn more about the Summer Olympics, go to **pressboxbooks.com/AllAccess**.

These links are routinely monitored and updated to provide the most current information available.

GLOSSARY

captain
A player who serves as the leader of a team.

dynasty
A team that has an extended period of success, usually winning multiple championships in the process.

endurance
The ability to keep doing something for a long time.

era
A period of time in history.

modern
Relating to the recent past.

professional
Paid to do something as a job.

racism
Hatred or mistreatment of people because of their skin color or ethnicity.

routine
The performance of a series of skills in gymnastics.

stereotypes
Overly simple and harmful ideas of how all members of a certain group are.

versatility
The ability to do a number of things well.

INDEX